# BE FRUITFUL and MULTIPLY

## Steven & Helen Anderson

Be Fruitful and Multiply

# BE FRUITFUL AND MULTIPLY

## Steven & Helen Anderson

# CONTENTS

# FOREWORD

In the realm of Christian leadership, where familiarity often breeds complacency, Steven and Helen Anderson stand as beacons of inspiration. Their latest book, "Be Fruitful and Multiply," not only bears witness to their unwavering commitment to pioneering the unknown but also serves as a timely guide for those navigating the currents of a new epoch.

In an age where settling into the known is a temptation, the Andersons defy the norm, demonstrating a tenacious spirit that continues to listen, adapt, and faithfully tread into uncharted territory. "Be Fruitful and Multiply" isn't just a book; it's a testament to a life lived in perpetual readiness for the 'new thing 'that God is orchestrating.

As we step into a season of reformation, this book emerges as a vital companion, offering practical insights firmly rooted in New Testament Christianity. Steven and Helen's journey becomes a roadmap for those seeking to embrace change with grace, navigating the uncharted waters of a transforming era.

Refreshingly accessible yet profoundly resonant, "Be Fruitful and Multiply" presents essential theology in a way that invites personal application. It doesn't prescribe a rigid model but, instead, beckons readers to explore the new wineskin that the Holy Spirit is pouring out in these reformation times.

In the hands of the Andersons, theology becomes not just a study but a lived experience—a call to fruitful multiplication, a summons to embrace the unexplored, and a testament to the enduring spirit of radical pioneers. May the wisdom within these pages inspire many to embark on their own transformative journeys.

Steve Uppal
All Nations
February 2024

# INTRODUCTION

In the beginning, God created. He created people and he blessed them. Then he spoke to them. He gave them permission to produce and reproduce, to be fruitful and multiply. God wanted more of them. A tragedy would occur and instead of the blessing a curse would fall on their lives and the ground around them. But there was a plan for redemption. It would take many centuries to form a people from whom the Redeemer would come. He came to break the curse, undo its effects, and restore the favour and blessing of God. He would bring forth a new creation – people re-born of his Spirit. He would bless them, appoint them, and anoint them so that once again they could be fruitful and multiply.

We have been redeemed and are being re-formed into the likeness of our Redeemer, the Son of God. He is the firstborn among many brothers and sisters (Romans 8:29). He wants more of us! He has designed us to carry his presence, the Father's glory, that the glory of the Lord might cover the earth.

In this short book, we are asking the question 'What will it take?' What will it take for us to become truly fruitful? What will it take to see a multiplying of our lives and believing communities? Hopefully, the following chapters will offer some signposts towards what it will take, signposts that may lead us along some unfamiliar paths (and some familiar ones), and make some new maps of the missional activity of a people filled with the Spirit of Jesus.

# 1

# RAISING EXPECTATION

*Expect great things from God; attempt great things for God*

William Carey, Missionary to India

## WHAT DO YOU SEE?

God asks this simple yet stretching question of both the prophets Jeremiah (1:11) and Zechariah (4:2). He is still asking it of those who have a willingness to listen, to look, and to learn. What do you see? What do you perceive? Jesus issues an invitation and a challenge to us: "Look, I tell you, lift up your eyes, and see that the fields are white for harvest" (John 4:35b). Here, we find a threefold emphasis:

'look'

'lift up your eyes'

'see.'

We can look but sometimes stare blankly and not notice anything. We must press through to deliberately lift our eyes with intention and purpose. As we do this we begin to truly see beyond what we've seen.

Again, he says, "The harvest is plentiful, but the labourers are few. Therefore, pray earnestly to the Lord of the harvest, to send out labourers into his harvest" (Luke 10:2). We are called to raise our sights to see with the eyes of Jesus, to see as he sees.

But what do we see? Are these fields ripe around about us or is there little evidence of that? What did the disciples see as Jesus was addressing them? What does Jesus see?

**HOW DO WE RESPOND TO THIS INVITATION AND CHALLENGE?**

The Apostle John, in Revelation 4:1, declares what he saw: "A door standing open in heaven"! There was an invitation to see and behold, an invitation that still stands. An invitation to 'come up here' to a different vantage point. John looked and beheld, not with a casual glance but a steady gaze into heaven. John continues in verse two to say "at once I was in the Spirit." He moves beyond his natural abilities and capacity, beyond his natural sight to see and hear in the Spirit.

**Look and see:** We can look but fail to see. Our eyes will often see what we expect to see based on our previous understanding and experience. We must look to see what we have not yet seen. If we are to see as Jesus sees then we first must lift our gaze upon him. To gaze on his beauty, to wonder and worship, as we lift our eyes to heaven seeing the Lamb upon the throne. To have our hearts enthralled with the Lamb who was slain, who has conquered, and who reigns! As we worship the true and living One, we begin to gain his perspective.

**Listen and hear:** We can listen but fail to truly hear due to a lack of attention or our presumptions and assumptions. Jesus cautions us to be careful how we listen (Luke 8:18), not just what or who we listen to. David says, "You have given me an open ear" (Psalm 40:6), which literally means you have dug open my ears! We have heard so many words, formed so many opinions, and have become at times set in our limited understanding that we need our ears dug open to truly hear in the Spirit.

**Learn and understand:** We can learn things – facts, information, and ideas from other people, but not truly understand. To understand what the Lord is revealing we may need to unlearn some old ways of thinking. This is a significant challenge that requires the renewing of the spirit of our minds (Ephesians 4:23), that is not just what we think, but how we think, in a new manner, from a different perspective, to see Jesus, see ourselves in and through him, and see the world in the light of Christ.

Unless we are born again of the Spirit, we cannot see the kingdom of God (John 3:3). But being born anew of the Spirit of God we can now see the kingdom and are called to seek the kingdom. The more that you seek the more you will see, and the more you see the more you will have a desire to seek even more.

## RAISING OUR BAR TO WHERE JESUS HAS SET IT

We can receive a fresh expectation based on God's Word and Spirit and not limited by our past experience. God-given expectation energises us, stirring our hearts and shaking off the dust of weariness. Receive a fresh excitement in the reading of Scripture with a mind opened to understand (Luke 24:45), and the veil lifted from any dullness of heart (Mark 6:52). Address the fear of disappointment and respond to God's appointment (John 15:16). Receive a fresh appointing from Jesus that will cast off the clothing of past disappointment and address the fear of future disappointment.

Let the words of Jesus raise our bar to where he sets it, not to where we might have lowered it based on our experiences. Jesus says, "The harvest is plentiful!" It is time to get ready and fully prepared. Expectation will lead to preparation. If you invite someone to your home for dinner and you fully expect they will come then you will prepare for their visit. You will tidy the house, cook the food, and set the table. If we are not preparing it is because we are not expectant. The living words and Spirit of Jesus will truly motivate us, creating momentum within us, and bringing forth a movement from among us.

**Seeing beyond ourselves and our previous horizons**

The Spirit of the Lord comes upon us to expand us to lead us into the greater expanse of God's kingdom. He brings revelation, dreams, and visions to draw us beyond ourselves and to expand our understanding. He comes to enlarge our hearts so that we might enlarge our steps.

**Seeing beyond our perceived restrictions and seeing into his spacious land for us**

I was woken one night by what appeared to me as a voice saying, 'You have cursed yourselves as a poor church!' This authoritative statement was not to be debated but did require a response. At the time I was pastoring in a small church in one of my city's more deprived areas. I took this 'word' and shared it with the three elders in the church. One by one they recognised how we had done this. Over the years people had often made statements that we'd always struggle financially as a church. We had in truth cursed ourselves, that is put a restriction around ourselves, hemming us in. Many of our restrictions are self-made! In response, we gathered the people, repented, broke the curse, and trusted God for a new freedom. We had been receiving an annual grant payment for many years from our denomination which covered around half of my salary. We wrote to them thanking them for their support, but now asking them to stop this grant as we are no longer a poor church! They duly obliged, and the next few months saw us not only meet every payment, including my full salary but have an excess that enabled a greater expansion of the ministry.

We can easily trap ourselves, fencing ourselves into our limitations when the Lord wants to expand us into a spacious place.

**Seeing beyond any past grievances and into his abundant grace**

We can all experience disappointment, pain, hurt, and relational fallout. The question is how are we going to respond. People can give offence but you don't have to take it! Many have been trapped in past grievances allowing the words or actions of another to have influence and even control over their life. Such grievances shrink our hearts and restrict our possibilities. Thankfully Jesus comes full of grace and truth. He forgives all our sins and enables us to forgive even as we are forgiven. As we receive more of his abundant grace we can extend this grace to others, past, present, and future. We can choose Christ's way and develop an 'unoffendable heart' where our sense of value is based on our relationship with Jesus and not affected by what other people do and say.

**Seeing beyond our small thinking and into the expansions of the mind of Christ**

We can be fooled into thinking we know a lot more than we actually do. The truth is as we go through life, we become more aware of how little we really know. There is so much more that is beyond us, that which 'no eye has seen, nor ear heard, nor the heart of man imagined.' Yet God has and is revealing through the Spirit to those who are looking and listening, for we have the mind of Christ available to us (see 1 Corinthians 2:9-16). Education and information can take us so far but the revelation and wisdom of the Holy Spirit can introduce us to a vast expansion of understanding in the realms of God's kingdom, and thereby what is and can be possible for those of us who believe.

**Seeing beyond how we have done things and into new pathways**

The familiar has a pull on most of us. To know where we are and have a sense of knowing what we are doing can be comforting. But if we are to see more than we have yet seen we must go to places we have not been. There are unfamiliar paths to be travelled as we go a way we may not have been before. This requires steps of faith, and trusting God for the next step without a map. We can feel vulnerable, even disorientated on these paths, but if we are prepared to let go of the seeming security of the familiar there is great reward to be discovered on the unfamiliar pathways.

**Seeing beyond our capabilities and into his power and glory (Ephesians 3:20)**

We cannot measure our possibilities by our natural capabilities. Yes, we have limited capacity in some ways but there is the game changer of 'the power at work within us.' Paul's prayer found in Ephesians 3:16-21 is about strengthening and stretching our inner being so that Christ would dwell in our hearts by faith. There is a dynamic at work within us that is beyond us. We have limited time and physical energy, but we have the presence and power of the Spirit who instructs our hearts even as we sleep, who prays through us in ways beyond our words, and who releases the words and works of God's kingdom that have a transformational effect. Seeing beyond means coming to a realisation of who is at work in us and releasing his life to flow through us.

**WHAT WILL IT TAKE?**

This is the simple, yet profound and vital question that we must be asking if we are to move from seeing something (vision) to actualising it where it becomes on earth as it is in heaven.

**Raise the bar by taking hold of these keys for a plentiful harvest:**

**Expectant vision:** Seeing more of the beauty and the fullness of the Lord and seeing beyond with him. Seeing with his eyes, his perspective, and from his vantage point. Allowing expectancy to grow within us we become pregnant (expectant) with the realities of heaven.

**Experiencing God's delight in us:** This expectation is borne out of our relationship with the Lord and grows within us as this relationship is nurtured. Everything else flows out from this relationship as expressions of God's life in us through his Spirit and word. Knowing his delighting in us and delighting ourselves in the Lord will sustain us through the battles for breakthroughs that are to come. We experience his affirming and affectionate love, his choosing of us, and his favour on us as his beloved ones.

**Expressing delight:** As we experience the love and delight of the Lord, we respond by expressing our delight in the Lord, and in the life and role that he has given us, even when the road is difficult or in times of waiting. As we give expression to this delight our appreciation of the Lord increases in our hearts. There will also be a maturing of this delight as we give expression even in the dark valleys of life. We have known much of God's goodness and favour but also walked through many valleys of depression, grief, and loss. Engaging in a faith expression of love to the Lord in all seasons develops the breadth and length and height and depth of love that surpasses knowledge (see Ephesians 3:18-19).

**Extraordinary prayer:** Proceeding from this relationship of delight come several important expressions of the ministry of Christ in and through us. Prayer is one such key expression. We learn to pray in and with the Spirit, not just our own cries but the very groans of the Spirit of God within us. We come to a greater understanding of praying in the name of Jesus, representing him, moving in his delegated authority, and calling forth on earth what the Lord has already done, that is as it is in heaven. We don't necessarily need more prayer with more words, but a greater comprehension and exercise of the authority Christ has given to us in prayer.

**Equipping the saints:** This is the great purpose of the ministry gifts of apostles, prophets, evangelists, shepherds, and teachers (Ephesians 4:11-12) making those around them in the community of believers fit for kingdom purposes. Here the people of God are restored, trained, and aligned, and there will be an activating and releasing of them to function fully in their callings and ministries.

**Extreme generosity:** A generous spirit is a necessary value in a move of God where we give away and release what he gives us. This will include giving financially, and also in serving, and in hospitality with open hearts and open homes. It will be expressed in forgiving all who wrong us or speak ill of us. It will show through how we release people and resources, at times giving away our best.

**Exercising authority:** As we dwell under the authority of the Lord over our lives, we will exercise Christ's authority over all demons and the domain of darkness. This comes out of a recognition of the authority Jesus has delegated to us and in submission to his authority over us. The battle lines are being drawn but we do not wage war as the world does or in the flesh. We war from a heart of worship, being continually clothed in Christ's righteousness so that the evil one will have no hold on us. We fight in humility and dependence on the Lord, not out of any presumption or pride.

**Explosion of signs and wonders:** The power of the Spirit is given that we might be witnesses to Jesus, the Risen One. This will many times be aided by miracles and healings as it was in the book of Acts with signs, wonders, and miracles increasing through the many not just a few, and into our communities and not kept in 'church services.' The apostles did many signs and wonders regularly among the people (Acts 5:12), but so also did Stephen (Acts 6:8), and then Philip (Acts 8:6) as the word spread and the mission expanded. We need an increase today of signs that point the way to Jesus and wonders that make people wonder, shifting them from unbelieving positions to faith in Jesus Christ.

**Exciting witness:** As we become enthralled with the testimony of Jesus, and the accompanying signs of his kingdom are breaking out around us, we will find ourselves explaining what he has done and is doing right now and is able to do, where we cannot help but speak of what we have seen and heard (Acts 4:20). In this context of kingdom activity witnessing about Jesus is so much less threatening and intimidating, but much more natural and exciting.

**Exponential discipling and birthing of reproducible simple churches:** As we pray in and with the Spirit, and move out in the power and authority that the Lord grants to us we will see the releasing of a movement of multiplication as we reach and disciple people who can reach and disciple many more. From there we can see the forming of simple church life around those disciples with a view to those simple churches birthing many more of their kind.

We will explore these themes further in later chapters.

## FIRST FRUIT BECOMING A HARVEST

Where we have seen the first fruits, we will see a harvest. What has happened can happen again, and again. It is time to press beyond those first fruits into the increase of his kingdom. We thank God for what we have seen – salvations, healing, freedom, and other works, we recount these, not to dwell there but to spur us on to greater works. It is now time to put into place the requirements to steward a move of God's Spirit into the increase and fulness that he desires and not to stop short. Too often we have seen a start or a stirring, recounted great promise and prophecy, but not entered into fulfilment. It is time to press through.

## HOW DO WE BEGIN?

We begin by taking the first step! We continue by taking the next step!

We took such a step at the end of 1999. The Lord called us to 'step out the boat,' out the safety, security, and familiarity of pastoring a local church. We left the position, gave up the salary and the house that went with it and took a step of faith. Looking back, it was the most liberating step we've taken. It opened up new territory and new possibilities and led to so much more than we would have imagined.

But we had to take the first step first. We moved out as a family of five and rented a house. We had no set income, no promise of income, and the Lord clearly instructed us not to ask anyone for money! Over many years that followed we never asked anyone for anything yet we paid every expense and never had a penny of debt. People would contact us 'out of the blue' offering a gift or monthly support. We always had enough. We had been loosed to go on an adventure, filled with heavenly expectation, to run with what the Lord gave us to do. Over the years we pioneered a prayer ministry in our city, began and developed many healing rooms across Scotland and Ireland, and travelled to many nations to teach, preach, prophesy, equip the saints, and demonstrate the kingdom of God in healing, signs, and wonders.

We all have steps to take in response to the call of God. Your steps may be quite different from ours but they are all steps that will launch us into the greater purposes of God on earth today. As heavenly vision and expectation grip our hearts it will thrust us from the safe and familiar places into the wide-open adventure of the expansion of the kingdom of God on earth as it is in heaven.

# 2

# RAISING THE FOUNDATIONS

*Those from among you will rebuild the ancient ruins; You will raise up the age-old foundations; And you will be called the repairer of the breach, The restorer of the streets in which to dwell.*

Isaiah 58:12 (NASB)

As expectation rises and we raise our sights, we seek to break through and build in ways that will have a lasting impact. It is vital therefore that we build on the right and true foundation.

The New Testament uses different images for the church which is the people of God. Some of the main images are God's field, God's building (1 Corinthians 3:9), the body of Christ (1 Corinthians 12:13), a spiritual house and a holy priesthood (1 Peter 2:5), and God's family or household (Ephesians 2:19). In fact, the church as the family of God is constantly affirmed with the use of the terms brothers and sisters, mothers and fathers, and sons and daughters throughout the New Testament.

We will begin this chapter by taking the image of the church as God's building. This is not to imply in any way that the church is a physical building which has been one of the greatest mistakes of western Christianity. It is to show that the family or people of God are built up in the same way that a building structure is by starting with a sure foundation. This foundation is a Person, Jesus Christ.

"For no man can lay a foundation other than that which is laid, which is Jesus Christ"

1 Corinthians 3:11

We build our lives on the foundation of Jesus Christ, the eternal Son of God, and we build by faith in him. The essentials of our faith in Christ are our core beliefs, which will lead to foundational values (what is truly important, necessary, and non-negotiable) and foundational practices that we build all else on.

We need lives and communities built on this one foundation which is the full provision of Christ Jesus. We need to know and recognise what he has done for us and made available to us. This goes beyond knowing about him. We must apprehend, appropriate, and apply his grace in all its truth (see Colossians 1:6). To apprehend is to understand and take hold of, even as he takes hold of us. To appropriate means to make this our own, and then we must apply his provision, which is to work this through into our whole life.

**SEVEN FOUNDATIONAL PILLARS IN CHRIST:**

*Wisdom has built her house; she has hewn her seven pillars.*
Proverbs 9:1

**What his death provided:** Jesus is the Passover Lamb, the Lamb of God who takes away the sin of the world. God has provided through Jesus' death on the cross the means to the forgiveness of sin so that we might be reconciled to God and made right with him. In Christ Jesus we have the grace of the New Covenant, a covenant relationship with God, whereby he has committed himself to us, to make us into the likeness of his Son (Romans 8:29). We have been brought into eternal union with Christ and the means to live in freedom and fullness of life. Our faith and hope rests on the completed work of Christ – 'it is finished!'

**What he won:** He has won the ultimate victory! He is risen and death is vanquished, and now all his enemies are under his feet. We are witnesses of the resurrection. In baptism, we are buried with him as we have died to the 'old life' in Adam and rise as new creations in Christ to live a new life. We stand in his victory where everything is possible to the one who believes.

**What he inaugurated:** Jesus introduced and brought in the kingdom of God, that is God's good, life-giving reign over all the destructive forces of sin, sickness, demons, and death. This kingdom has come and still comes towards its fulfilment. We live in his kingdom now in order to bring more of his kingdom rule from heaven to earth. Like Jesus, we announce the good news of the kingdom breaking into the domain of darkness in this world, and we demonstrate the kingdom through signs and wonders.

**What he gave:** He pours out the wonderful gift of the Holy Spirit, the Father's promise for us. The One we walk with, are taught by, led by, empowered with, and who anoints us with fresh oil. We must be filled with and fully embrace the activation of the Spirit, his work, and gifts in our life experience. The receiving of the gift or baptism of the Holy Spirit is a definite and dynamic experience in our lives resulting in expressions of his life, revelation, and power in and through us.

**What he modelled:** Jesus modelled for us his life and ways that are expressed in his relationship with the Father and the Spirit, in relating to all people, in speaking words of life, in healing, and freeing people from darkness, and in demonstrating the overarching authority of God's kingdom. He modelled how to live as a true Son of the true Father. He now calls us to follow him and his example. This example also means, like him, laying down our supposed rights (see Philippians 2:5-8), letting go of our attempts at self-preservation, and giving of ourselves to the purposes of God.

**Who he appointed:** While Jesus has appointed all his followers to bear much fruit, he has appointed apostles and prophets as foundational ministries in the church to aid in raising up the whole body (Ephesians 2:20). Jesus is the cornerstone, the essential building block that all else must align with, and as the whole body is built up, we need these foundational ministry gifts of apostles and prophets to operate fully in the Spirit of Christ. The lack of recognition and therefore lack of operation of these gifts in much of church history must be put right in these days. Apostles and prophets with the heart of the Father will raise up sons and daughters who will speak with the authority of Christ's kingdom.

**What he has given access to:** We now have access to the throne of grace and the Father's favour and blessing. Jesus is the way to the Father that we might live as beloved sons and daughters. We have every spiritual blessing in Christ (Ephesians 1:3). We have access to the gate of heaven (Genesis 28:17), and are appointed to bring the realities of heaven forth upon the earth.

From these foundational truths, we must allow a fundamental shift in our understanding so we can enter into all the amazing benefits of such a great salvation. As we come in confession and repentance, receiving full forgiveness so we can live with nothing to hide! As we receive and live by the grace of God, we have nothing to prove. There is no longer any need for pretence and no place for performance! As we are rooted in love, in the Beloved One, this perfect love drives out all fear. This is true freedom and this is the fullness of life that Jesus gives (John 10:10), living with nothing to hide, nothing to prove, and nothing ultimately to fear.

As we raise up these 'age-old' foundations we discern what is truly important, that is our core values.

**SEVEN CORE VALUES:**

**Presence of God:** Moses said that he would not go up from where he was unless the Lord's presence (his face) was with them (Exodus 33:15). God's presence with us, where the Lord walks among us is essential (Leviticus 26:12). This is our distinctive, Emmanuel, God with us. In his presence is fullness of joy (Psalm 16:11), and in his presence, we find peace, healing of our souls, and much more.

**Passion for Jesus:** We must never lose our first love but keep the fire of holy passion burning within our hearts. Full of the growing appreciation of who Jesus is and what he has done for us, passion for him will continually fill us. As we behold him in holy awe, the imprint of sin, the flesh, and the world fade away, and we are increasingly impressed with Jesus, releasing his fragrance everywhere.

**Power of the Spirit coupled with the Word of God:** We receive power when the Holy Spirit comes upon us, a power that is necessary to enable us to be effective witnesses to Jesus. There is never a choice between the Spirit and the Word of God, but we highly esteem them both. The Word and Spirit complement each other as the Word releases the activity of the Spirit, and the Spirit's activities confirm the Word of God.

**People:** The church is the people of God and is therefore highly relational. We value people, each and every one of them, above programmes or the performance of services. We value one another for who we are in the Lord and enable one another to function in the calling of God in each of our lives.

**Participation:** We value the participation of all. We don't seek to build an audience for one person's ministry but to release people into their ministries. We believe in and value the priesthood of all believers, which has been a key doctrine from the Reformation. However, it has not always been implemented. We have often deferred to and relied upon 'professional clergy' when in truth all of us who are in Christ can hear his voice, follow his commands, and bear much fruit.

**Practice of his commands:** Jesus' commands are to be practiced not merely discussed and debated. They are not complex nor are they burdensome, but clear and life-giving. We need to live out an obedience-based discipleship. We grow most fully as we do what he has told us. This practice is not as a means of gaining God's favour but an expression of living in his favour.

**Purpose of God:** Finally, we recognise we are a people with purpose, with the upward call of God on our lives. That purpose is to crown Jesus as Lord in all we do. In the way we relate to him, to one another, and in making him known in all our land. He gives us great commands and a great commission.

These core beliefs and values result in foundational practices that are of great importance: worship with praise and thanksgiving, praying in the Spirit, dwelling deeply in the Scriptures, generosity in giving, making room for the Spirit of God to move among us, and following the commands of Jesus primarily loving the Lord with everything and loving one another.

**SEVEN COMMANDS OF JESUS:**

While Jesus gave many instructions and commands here are seven key commands that help summarise his teaching. Following his commands is an outworking of faith where we are enabled by his grace as his Spirit increasingly envelops and permeates our whole being. These commands are not put on us from without but rise from a God-given desire in our hearts. Obedience is not forced or contrived but overflows from our hearts when we delight in the Lord. Jesus' commands are invitations to live as he lived.

**Love the Lord your God (Matthew 22:27-38):** To love him who first loved us, which is what makes loving him possible. We respond to the revelation of his love which is 'poured into our hearts by the Holy Spirit' (Romans 5:5). We love him with everything we are and have.

**Love your neighbour (one another) (Matthew 22:39; John 13:34-35):** Out of the love of God and loving God, will flow a love for other people. The love of God drives out all fear, including the great and crippling fear of rejection that often hinders us from expressing love to others. In obedience we show love to one another in the family of God, to our neighbours, and even to our enemies (Matthew 5:44). The love of Christ crosses all barriers and boundaries.

**Seek first the kingdom of God (Matthew 6:33):** Jesus calls us to this priority as a way of life. Rather than being concerned and consumed by the things of this world with its many worries and anxieties, we focus first and foremost on his life-giving kingdom rule and find that in that every other need is met. This seeking leads us into a deeper life of prayer, beyond just our needs, into calling forth his kingdom will on earth as it is in heaven.

**Give generously (Luke 6:37-38; Mark 10:45):** We value generosity which must be expressed through a heart of giving. We give, not grudgingly or half-heartedly but in full measure. We give and forgive as a life practice. We give ourselves, laying down our comforts, our wants, and our selfish ambitions. We discover the joy of giving, that it is 'more blessed to give than to receive' (Acts 20:35).

**Announce the good news (Luke 4:18-19):** Everyone wants and needs to hear some good news! And we have the best news which is the victory of Jesus over all darkness and destruction. Jesus sends us as heralds announcing the good news of the kingdom of God. We need to allow this good news to permeate our whole lives so that it will overflow from our hearts. The Spirit supplies confidence, freedom, and boldness to us to speak this message of new life.

**Heal the sick and free the oppressed (Mark 3:14-15; Luke 9:1-2):** Alongside this announcement, Jesus sends his followers to heal the sick and drive out demons. These 'signs' accompanied Jesus' ministry and that of the church in Acts. They have been sadly lacking through much of the history of the Western church. In faith, we receive Christ's anointing and authority and will find its outworking only as we step out in obedience.

**Disciple others in all of this (Matthew 28:19-20):** Jesus' final command is to raise up others as he raised up disciples. To baptise them into Christ and disciple them in all these commandments of Jesus. This brings us full circle and begins new circles of true life in the Spirit. We can only teach others by demonstrating our own desire to be obedient to the commands of Jesus.

The wise man builds his house on a rock, a solid foundation, by hearing and putting into practice the words of Jesus (Matthew 7:24). While we will personally build our lives on this Rock, so we must rebuild a community of faith, worship, and mission. It is only when we are living and building on the foundation of Jesus Christ, not only doctrines about him but also our relationship with him, that we will build again the ancient ruins and be ready for a great ingathering of believers into Christ's church who will live as devoted followers of Jesus. Then together we will 'repair the breach' and 'restore pathways with dwelling places.'

If the foundations are not right or cracked, then no matter what we build on top of them it will eventually crumble and collapse. It is vitally important to check that our foundations are true and solid before we move on any further.

# 3

# RAISING UP SONS AND DAUGHTERS

*The Spirit himself bears witness with our spirit that we are*

*children of God*

Romans 8:16

A desperate father comes to Jesus seeking his help and healing for his sick daughter. Indeed, she is near death. He waits while Jesus brings healing to a woman who has been suffering a long-term infirmity. His heart begins to sink as he sees messengers arriving from his house. Their faces look grave and they have the worst news this father could imagine: "Your daughter is dead." Jesus is undeterred by the news and encourages hope and faith as he declares, "Do not be afraid, only believe and keep believing" If this father,

Jairus, could believe for his daughter's healing then could he not also believe Jesus to raise her back to life?

Jesus goes with him taking his inner circle of followers, Peter, James, and John. He encounters the mourners weeping and wailing, and Jesus announces that the child is not dead but asleep! The mourning turns to mocking at the Lord's outrageous comments. Putting these unbelieving ones outside, Jesus takes his three men and the father and mother into the room where the girl lies. He takes her by the hand, raises her back to life, and tells them to feed her! This account, found in Mark 5:21-43 reveals what Jesus can do as he brings the life-giving kingdom of God to overcome even the rule of death. We can see in this passage an illustration of how the power and name of Jesus can raise the sleeping church, the sons and daughters of the kingdom, back to full life. Some see the church as dying and in some places dead. But Jesus says that she is only sleeping. Yes, there is a spiritual malaise that has infected her but there is hope and we need only to believe. Out of that faith, and in Jesus' name, we can bring healing, raise to new life, and give her something nourishing to feed upon.

## SONS AND DAUGHTERS

Jesus came and revealed God as Father. God the Father's declaration over Jesus at his baptism, and then repeated on the Mount of Transfiguration is: 'This is my Beloved Son' (see Matthew 3:17; 17:5). God the Father raises up, and represents himself through people, through sons and daughters. Any forms and structures we have must only be to aid sons and daughters to function fully in their God-given calling. God puts His Spirit in people, not structures or buildings. He pours new wine into new creation people. Sometimes we have raised up 'ministers' even professionals. We have our identity in a job, or a function, or even a position, but not in sonship. Sons (and daughters) will function in ministry, but it must be from an abiding place of relationship with and naming by the Father. We are sons who serve and obey the Father, not striving for approval and acceptance, but out of love and delight in the One who delights in us his children. We need workers for the harvest, and we are called to serve, but the greatest worker and servant was the Son. The Father did not declare 'This is my beloved servant' but 'Beloved Son!' Only sons and daughters can reveal the heart of the Father. The world doesn't need to see our performance but the Father's heart of love.

We are described in many ways in Scripture, as bondservants, ambassadors, citizens of heaven, and much more, but first and foremost we have been given the right to become children of God.

When we realise and understand that we have been baptised into Christ, having died to our old life in Adam and been raised to new life in the Son, Christ Jesus, then we enter into the full relationship of sons and daughters to the Father and with the Holy Spirit even as Jesus related to them as he walked among us. We are raised up in love, having been named by the Father, and so we can walk as healthy, whole people in true integrity.

In the great prayer of Paul in Ephesians 3:14-21 we read that he prays to the Father who names us, thus giving us our identity, a true sense of who we really are. Identity is only realised in relationship. Paul is praying for the church as sons and daughters who will be strengthened by the Spirit of God within them. Sons and daughters who have Christ dwelling in their hearts, and therefore are rooted and grounded in love. This is a vital ingredient of a healthy relationship that our life, our heart, and the essence of our being will be truly rooted, implanted in, and therefore be grounded and established in the love of God. This enables us to grow up and stand up to full height in our God-given identity, knowing all the full dimensions of Christ. This can only be fully realised together. We cannot rise up to full sonship in isolation from other sons and daughters of the Father (see Ephesians 3:14-21).

As we together comprehend in our minds and hearts the love of the Son and grow in the experiential, relational knowledge of the Son of God, so we grow into maturity as sons and daughters (Ephesians 4:13). We are loved with an everlasting love from the beginning, even in our immaturity, but the Father does not want us to remain there but he raises us up as maturing sons and daughters who will function as fathers and mothers to others.

**FATHERS AND MOTHERS IN CHRIST**

The great need of our societies is for true fathers and mothers. Only those who have become healthy sons and daughters can truly function as these fathers and mothers in the kingdom, raising up many more sons and daughters. We don't need more managers or even teachers, but fathers and mothers (1 Corinthians 4:15).

As we move towards rebuilding the ruins, and forming healthy, life-giving communities of faith, we see that the essential building block is family. Those coming to faith must be born of the Spirit and born into a family. In families, you find identity, belonging, value, and purpose, and in families, you find mothers, fathers, sons, and daughters.

Jesus brings us to his Father who is now our Father. He brings us to hear the Father's voice speak over us, "This is my beloved son (daughter), with whom I am well pleased." We receive the Father's blessing, that is his naming, his permission to flourish and thrive, his calling us to be and become, and his releasing us from self-absorption to a world-transforming purpose. In the very beginning God blessed man and woman to be fruitful and to multiply (Genesis 1:28), and in his very last act before he ascended to heaven Jesus blessed his disciples for the same purpose (Luke 24:50-51).

**WHAT DO FATHERS AND MOTHERS IN THE KINGDOM DO?**

Fathers and mothers affirm, name, and give identity. They call forth and bless just as the Father has done for them. We can only give what we have received from heaven. As we truly know the blessing of the Father, we are blessed to be a blessing to others. The following list expands and explains how this heavenly blessing is imparted and enables sons and daughters to be fruitful and multiply as they themselves become mothers and fathers.

Fathers and mothers train, nurture, confront, correct, and release. They train their sons and daughters in how to live well, nurturing their gifts and abilities. Because they love they are not afraid to confront wrongs and bring healthy correction. And because they want to see their sons and daughters truly flourish, they are prepared to let them go at the right time.

Fathers and mothers bring security, but not by controlling. They allow freedom but without chaos. They create relational places where sons and daughters can expand. Too often insecure leaders, not knowing the true heart of the Father, have sought to bring growth to people and the church but have used controlling and even manipulative methods. These methods may manufacture impressive short-term results but will not bear lasting fruit.

Fathers and mothers give opportunities for sons and daughters to increase and go beyond where they themselves have gone. They delight in their children's success. They want to see a generational increase.

Fathers and mothers give permission to flourish and succeed, and to be fruitful. Many people have lived under such control and even oppression that they are desperately seeking permission to express themselves. We have often found that a simple permission-giving prayer over a person has brought incredible release.

Fathers and mothers give birth to new life and to new expressions of the kingdom of God on earth. They create opportunities for their sons and daughters to step into.

Fathers and mothers don't use people; they invest in them. Too many people have felt used for someone else's purpose. We don't use people to serve our ministry but invest wisely in them to release their own ministry in due course.

Fathers and mothers represent and live out God's heart; they don't just talk about the things of God but display him. They haven't just read about God or listened to what others have taught, but they have sat close to the heart of the Father.

Fathers and mothers bring character alongside giftedness. Great giftedness can bring fast growth but it will falter sooner or later if there is not the character to sustain it.

Fathers and mothers have had their own character developed through their walk with the Lord in all the seasons of life, and bring the value of character that brings out the best in gifting.

Fathers and mothers bring a rounded and full picture, being concerned for the whole family. They don't have favourites but want the best for everyone.

Fathers and mothers bring wisdom to revelation. We can all receive revelation from the Spirit, even when we are immature in the faith. Too much revelation without the accompanying wisdom can actually be a problem for us.

In the church, we are often seeking to develop and raise up leaders when we may need to raise up mothers and fathers who can truly lead like Jesus out of relationship with the Father. We have adopted much language from the business world into the life of the church. Language creates culture and we are in danger of creating a business culture with CEO's and managers. We are not an organisation but a living organism. We are a worshipping family on mission together. We are sons and daughters, brothers and sisters, and mothers and fathers who will bear the family resemblance as we worship the Father and Son, and remain impressed with Jesus so he can make his true impression on us. The Spirit also testifies within us that we are God's children, producing in us the deep cry of 'Abba, Father!'

# 4

# RECOVERING APOSTOLIC MISSION

*God wants to disrupt us and bring us back to the life and*
*mission of Jesus*

Steve Addison, Acts and the Movement of God

We are the family of God, those who worship him by the Spirit, who glory in Christ Jesus and put no confidence in our own merits (Philippians 3:3). We are people who love the Lord, love one another, and look out to the white harvest fields to bring the Good News to those in darkness. We are a missionary people. But what is the mission or the co-mission, and why call it 'apostolic'?

We want to build on the true foundation and we also want to be sure we are following the true mission that Jesus gave his disciples, whom he designated apostles. It is time to re-read the Scriptures, especially those where Jesus sends out his disciples such as Matthew 28:16-20 and Luke 24:44-53 alongside the book of Acts. The apostles are the sent ones, they are on a mission and they are taking others with them. The ascended Christ has given his church the foundational gifts of apostles and prophets. The prophet provides the fuel and the apostle provides the thrust for mission. After all, Jesus said to ask for workers to be sent out or literally thrust out into the harvest field (Luke 10:2). That fuel and thrust will carry many, many workers into the ripe fields.

**MATTHEW 28:16-20**

Jesus starts with just eleven men. They worship him though some of them have doubts. Doubts don't disqualify us but as we acknowledge them and work them through in prayer, the Lord will strengthen our faith. Jesus states his absolute authority in heaven and on earth, and therefore his authorisation of them as his representatives. He sends them, and as they go, he commissions them to disciple all peoples, baptising them into his life, and teaching them to obey, not just acknowledge all his commands. We need obedience-based discipleship that leads us out and actions his commands rather than endless discussion of them that goes around in circles. Finally, he gives the promise that he will always be with them.

It is vitally important that we come to understand Christ's absolute authority in all things, and the resulting authorisation he gives to us to fulfil his commission. Being authorised by the author of life gives us confidence and certainty. This mission of the kingdom is not something we have invented; it is a heavenly vision.

## LUKE 24:44-53

Jesus appears to his disciples over a period of time giving various instructions. Here he reminds them that he is the fulfilment of all that was written in the Law and Prophets. He opens their minds further to more fully understand the Scriptures of which we see evidence of this new understanding in Peter's preaching on the day of Pentecost. Jesus presents the gospel, that is that he died, was buried, and rose again (see 1 Corinthians 15:3-4), and commissions them to proclaim repentance for the forgiveness of sins throughout all nations. He instructs them to wait in the city until they receive the necessary gift and clothing with power from the Holy Spirit. He blessed them – the last thing he does before ascending, and this was the first thing God did when he created man (Genesis 1:28) – and they responded by worshipping him and continually praising God.

We then see the outworking and unfolding of this commissioning in the book of Acts as Jesus announces that they will receive power when the Holy Spirit comes upon them, and they will be his witnesses from where they are to the very ends of the earth. The book of Acts follows the story of this witness in the power of the Spirit through the likes of Peter, John, Stephen, Philip, Barnabas, and Paul as the Good News spreads widely and at times wildly. If there is one word that might be used to describe the Book of Acts it would be 'unstoppable.' Despite persecution and opposition of many kinds, the testimony of Jesus continues unabated. It still does today!

### SIX STAGES IN THE BOOK OF ACTS

The book of Acts unfolds the story of the spread of the message of Jesus throughout the known world. The whole narrative is the expansion of verse eight of chapter one: "But you will receive power when the Holy Spirit comes upon you, and you will be my witnesses in Jerusalem and in all Judea and Samaria, and to the end of the earth."

We can be part of this narrative today as we keep receiving the power to witness that comes from the Holy Spirit.

**Stage 1:** The setting is in Jerusalem which we find in chapters 1-6 concluding with the statement in 6:7: "And the word of God continued to **increase**, and the number of disciples **multiplied greatly** in Jerusalem, and a **great many** of the priests became obedient to the faith."

This stage includes the wonderful happenings on the day of Pentecost as the Spirit is poured out and tongues of fire rest on every believer with the resulting sound filling the city. Many are drawn by this heavenly sign, the message of Jesus is proclaimed, and many respond in faith. What an awesome day! The church begins to form around the apostles as they teach the new believers. They meet regularly in public places and in homes, eating together, praying, and praising God. The numbers continue to grow as people come to faith. Signs, wonders, and miracles are happening, initially at the hands of the apostles. A most significant healing takes place by the temple gate and even more people respond to the message of new life in Jesus. The first opposition then comes, with threats to attempt to silence these men and women. In response the believers gather to pray, calling on the Lord to give them even more boldness to speak his word, while he brings forth more healings, signs, and wonders (See the key prayer of Acts 4:29-30). There is a fresh moving and filling of the Holy Spirit.

The new community of faith is flourishing with great displays of God's power and people's generosity. Issues arise that could hamper the work but are dealt with in decisive ways. The apostles continue to work many signs and wonders (Acts 5:12) and proclaim the good news. More opposition comes from without and some irritations arise within. To deal with the internal strife which we see in chapter six, the apostles raise up seven men to help with this ministry. Two notable ones are Stephen and Philip who begin to move in the power of the Spirit like the apostles had been doing. This section ends with the testimony and martyrdom of Stephen.

Up to this point, amazing works and wonders have taken place, and there has been significant growth of the believing community. But they have stayed in Jerusalem. There has been no mention of going beyond to other places as Jesus said they would do. Now a greater level of persecution breaks out which is spearheaded by a certain man called Saul who himself will become arguably the greatest missionary.

**Stage 2:** Here the message of Jesus spreads out to Judea, Samaria, and Galilee which concludes with chapter 9:31 stating: "So the church throughout Judea and Galilee and Samaria had peace and was being built up. And walking in the fear of the Lord and in the comfort of the Holy Spirit, it **multiplied**."

This spread begins as a result of the fierce opposition of the religious authorities. Philip goes to Samaria where he testifies in the power of the Spirit. As people see the signs of the kingdom in healing and casting out evil spirits, they pay close attention to Philip's message. A great work of God takes place before Philip is amazingly led by the Spirit to a desert road to connect with an Ethiopian eunuch.

The story shifts back to Saul (Paul) and the equally amazing turnaround in his life as he encounters the risen Lord Jesus. This brings a time of peace to the growing churches which have now spread through Judea, Samaria, and Galilee. The story is being partly fulfilled but there is still a long way to go.

**Stage 3:** Now the good news breaks into the Gentile world described in chapters 10-12 where huge boundaries and mindsets were crossed. This is summed up in 12:24 with the simple words: "But the word of God **increased** and **multiplied.**"

This begins with the Holy Spirit wonderfully orchestrating events around Peter and the household of a Roman centurion, Cornelius. Angelic visitation, heavenly vision, and the voice of the Spirit speaking bring about the connection that breaks the most significant boundary of the time between Jew and Gentile. These supernatural phenomena are to be expected when the Spirit is moving his people beyond where they have been and what they can see. These sorts of happenings are to be expected among us today. Peter's visit to Cornelius takes place around AD37 and causes no small stir in the main church base in Jerusalem. It has been groundbreaking and has opened something in the spirit realm. In Acts 11:19 we come back to those who had been scattered after the death of Stephen. It is now around AD42 and we find some men from Cyprus and Cyrene who go to Antioch and break out of the mould and begin speaking the message of Jesus to Hellenists, that is Greek-speaking non-Jews. This is clearly pleasing to the Lord, as his hand is with them in a special way, and a great number of people believe and turn to the Lord. The good news is now spreading towards the ends of the earth. In our day there are other barriers and boundaries that need to be broken through by those who will be led by the Spirit and step beyond with great courage.

The great mission base that the church of Antioch will become, is now being formed with Barnabas and Saul (Paul) as two key players.

**Stage 4:** This section records the missionary journeys of Paul and his teams, which begin in chapter 13, with a summary statement found in 16:5: "So the churches were strengthened in the faith, and they **increased** in numbers daily."

These great mission adventures begin in the place of worship, fasting, and prayer where the Holy Spirit speaks and directs. There doesn't seem much debate but more fasting, prayer, and the laying on of hands as these two pioneers are sent out. The following accounts tell of the great works and wonders of their mission, along with much opposition culminating with Paul being stoned and left for dead. The story even has a big falling out between Paul and Barnabas, but this results in more people being added to the apostolic teams. New maps are being made as the message of Jesus spreads into new lands.

**Stage 5:** Now the mission moves into Europe from chapter 16 onwards. This stage is summed up when Paul is in Ephesus and Acts 19:20 says: "So the word of the Lord continued to **increase** and prevail mightily."

Paul has visited and preached in many cities now. He would begin in the synagogue if there was one, and when they didn't fully embrace the message, he would move out to the Gentiles. His stay is short in some places, partly due to opposition, but he remains longer in Corinth and then longer still in Ephesus. While Antioch was the base Paul was sent out from and returned and reported to, Ephesus became a new centre for the widespread mission and birthing of churches. Here Paul develops what we will describe in the next chapter as an Apostolic Base Camp.

**Stage 6:** Finally, we move on to Rome where Paul may have finished his endeavours but the mission certainly did not stop - it's unstoppable! Here we have the concluding verses of the book which state in 28:30-31: "He lived there two whole years at his own expense, and welcomed all who came to him, proclaiming the kingdom of God and teaching about the Lord Jesus Christ with all boldness and without hindrance."

Paul travelled from Ephesus to Jerusalem before being arrested and spending much time under guard in Caesarea and then Rome. Most of the final chapters are taken up with his imprisonment and testifying before kings and governors which had been prophesied over him after his conversion (Acts 9:15). Though chained, Paul still testified freely and with great confidence. Indeed, the final words of the book of Acts state that he continued to proclaim the kingdom of God and teach about Jesus with all boldness and without hindrance.

Notice how often the words 'increase' and 'multiply' occur in the verses in each section. It is how it is meant to be and can be. The final words 'without hindrance' pronounce loudly that this message of the Risen Christ cannot be silenced or stopped.

**WHAT'S NEXT? WHAT STAGE IS SET FOR US?**

The Good News travelled out on new and unfamiliar paths. What are the unfamiliar paths that the Spirit is leading us on in the unstoppable mission of God to make Jesus known to the ends of the earth?

The apostolic mission is as a witness to Jesus and his resurrection and Lordship.

It is accompanied and driven forward by the power of the Holy Spirit through healings, miracles, signs, and wonders. These accompanying signs are needed every bit as much today as they ever were. Through this mission disciples come forth and simple churches comprised of these disciples are formed. This is not the end, but both disciples of Jesus and these communities of faith carry within their spiritual DNA the means to reproduce and multiply over and over again.

The stage is now set for us. It may be a very different-looking one to the first-century world of the Mediterranean basin. But God is still God and people are still people. The Spirit of God is still at work, calling, speaking, orchestrating, and moving in power. The message of Jesus is still highly relevant to every person. His grace and truth are still life-transforming. New maps are waiting to be drawn showing the spread of the good news of the kingdom and the birthplaces of many new communities of believers.

# 5

# RECREATING APOSTOLIC BASE CAMPS

*Enlarge the place of your tent, stretch your tent curtains wide, do not hold back; lengthen your cords, strengthen your stakes. For you will spread out to the right and to the left*

Isaiah 54:2-3 (NIV)

Not all the churches in the New Testament were alike. Even in the earliest days of the Book of Acts, we can see different models of church with different emphases. I believe there is a progression throughout Acts which we can trace primarily through the models of church in Jerusalem, Antioch, and Ephesus.

**The Jerusalem church** set the tone and had many great attributes as God moved among them and they saw a great increase (Acts 2:41-47). However, as we saw in the last chapter, they did not appear to actively engage in the full extent of Jesus' command to be His witnesses also in Judea, Samaria, and to the ends of the earth (Acts 1:8). It took persecution to scatter them and begin the spread outside of Jerusalem (Acts 8:1ff). Neither did they seem to be prepared to cross the divide into the Gentile world. This wouldn't start to happen until the great shift that takes place with Peter's vision and Cornelius' household in Acts 10.

After the first Gentiles came to faith there was still resistance and difficulty with this idea. However, some believers from Cyprus and Cyrene started speaking to Greeks where they saw great responsiveness (Acts 11:20-21). This was the start of the church in Antioch. True to its boundary-breaking foundations this church would become a missionary sending centre (Acts 13:1-3), and the home base for Paul. Going from and returning to Antioch, Paul and his companions started several churches in other cities. The Antioch church displayed several important features.

**FEATURES OF THE ANTIOCH CHURCH:**

1. It was established through breaking new ground (11:19-20). The way we start is often the way we go on unless we reach a plateau where we get stuck. As we break new ground in this day, we can create a platform for the breaking of more and more new territory.

2. They celebrated what God was doing (11:23). This begins with Barnabas, the son of encouragement, who was sent by the Jerusalem church to see what was happening in Antioch. Barnabas was a model of generosity, both in giving of his resources (Acts 4:36-37) and in his embracing of Paul (Acts 9:26-27). He sees the best in people and sees the best of what the Lord is doing in this place. He values Paul and goes and finds him in Tarsus and brings him to Antioch.

3. There was consolidating teaching (11:26). Barnabas and Paul spent considerable time teaching the people the word of God and the ways of Jesus. This teaching builds deep foundation blocks into the new work, and into the lives of many people.

4. They responded to prophetic words (11:27-30). They were open to words of prophecy from the Lord, not only hearing but responding in appropriate action. Sometimes we hear prophetic words and just wait and hope for their fulfilment without seeing that we have to respond and play our part in that fulfilment.

5. They exemplified extreme generosity in attitude and finance and people (11:29; 13:3). No doubt the generous spirit in Barnabas made a deep impression on the people here. Not only did they give of their money, but they also released two of their best for a wider ministry. As we hold on to what we have we will lose it in the kingdom. As we release and give away, we will be positioned to receive so much more.

6. They worshipped and fasted, ministering to the Lord (13:2). This was likely a regular practice and way of life for these prophets and teachers who were leading the work in Antioch. They looked to the Lord and gave to him first. This posture enabled them to receive his directions.

7. They listened to the Holy Spirit and followed his leading (13:2). And so, the Holy Spirit was able to speak clearly to them. They didn't waste any time but acted in accordance with what the Spirit had said. They may not have known what this would look like for Barnabas and Paul, but they stepped out in faith and obedience.

8. They released and sent out the best (13:3). It could easily have been their hope and ambition to keep these two mighty men of God in their midst. They could have looked to what would benefit and build their church. But instead, they release them without any apparent conditions. With a healthy release, good relationships can remain in place, and this must have been so as Paul and Barnabas returned again and again to Antioch.

Paul stayed for various lengths of time in different places – some very short, often due to persecution, others longer like Corinth for 18 months, and then Ephesus for around three years. It is **Ephesus that becomes a new base for Paul**. It is a base for equipping and sending out many to spread the good news and to start churches. The whole region heard the word of the Lord (Acts 19:10) while Paul remained in Ephesus. This city was a commercial centre where many would come to and go back again to their towns and villages. Some would have heard Paul, been converted, influenced, and equipped by him to go home and birth new works of God. Ephesus was a city with a major demonic stronghold, yet Paul brought great breakthroughs through extraordinary miracles (19:11) and exposing the occult practices.

**At Ephesus (Acts 19) Paul's apostolic ministry led to:**

**\*Believers being filled with the Holy Spirit, speaking in tongues and prophesying (v6).** Paul is very keen to ensure that these disciples have received the definite and dynamic gift of the Holy Spirit. He makes sure the bases are covered and the correct foundations are in place, baptising them in the name of Jesus. This is immediately followed by the impartation of the gift of the Spirit through the laying on of hands. The gift is not just a nice feeling but is clearly and substantially evidenced in these men speaking in tongues and prophesying in line with what happened at Pentecost.

**\*People are equipped to share the good news and start churches (v9-10).** Paul spent two years where he taught, reasoned, and equipped so many people that through them the whole region heard the word of the Lord. This would also include many demonstrations of the Spirit's power so that it is said that Paul did extraordinary miracles there.

**\*The loosening of the demonic stronghold over the city (v18-20; v23ff).** The miracles of healing and the casting out of evil spirits broke open the way for a greater work of deliverance and undoing the works of the devil. Many repent and get set free from the strong occult powers that dominated that city. Their sincerity is shown in the burning of their expensive books. This in turn shakes the demonic stronghold or principality over that area which was located in the worship of Artemis.

While the Antioch church was a key mission-sending base for a vast region, it is in Ephesus that Paul creates what we might term an Apostolic Base Camp. From here many come to faith and are equipped and released to spread the message of Jesus across a region and to birth new churches.

**WHAT IS A BASE CAMP?**

A base camp is a place from which mountaineering expeditions set out or from which a particular activity can be carried out. It is a place where food and general supplies are kept, providing shelter, supplies, and communications for those engaged in wide-ranging activities, such as exploring, reconnaissance, hunting, or mountain climbing. A base camp, like the one at Mount Everest, also functions as a staging post where climbers become acclimatised to altitude before continuing their ascent.

So, an Apostolic Base Camp provides these same types of resources – feeding on the word of God; equipping people for the works of the kingdom of God; providing shelter, healing, and restoration; being a connection point for continued communication; and acclimatising people for re-entering the mission arena.

**WHAT COULD THIS LOOK LIKE FOR US?**

Base camps can be very simple places with a few tents set up. They are flexible and moveable, not requiring great expense or buildings. Paul used the hall of Tyrannus in Ephesus where he taught and equipped many people for mission and birthing churches. We can use a simple meeting place, maybe moving to somewhere else when necessary. It doesn't have to be large to be effective. It's about preparing God's people well so they can be fruitful and multiply.

**THE GIFTS OPERATING HERE**

These base camps are places where ministry gifts operate to equip the saints. We often focus on the five gifts of

Ephesians 4:11, but there is a similar but more expanded list found in 1 Corinthians 12:28: "And God has appointed in the church first apostles, second prophets, third teachers, then miracles, then gifts of healing, helping, administrating, and various kinds of tongues." The base camp is a valid expression of church where three of the five ministry gifts of Ephesians 4 are again listed – apostles, prophets, and teachers. Evangelists and shepherds (pastors) are not listed here, and these gifts may be more suited to simple churches that are birthed out from the base camps. It is in the local, simple church as a family on mission together that we reach out to people who don't yet know Jesus, and provide pastoral care and strength to each other.

The order of the gifts listed in 1 Corinthians 12:28 does not represent a hierarchy but an order of function and priority. If you don't have apostolic gifting then none of the others will operate to their full potential. The apostle has the gift to gather, to see the bigger picture, to bring out the best in the other giftings, and to release people beyond where they have been and into the greater works of God. The prophet is so necessary to bring fuel to the fire, to encourage, warn, and correct the course. The teacher then equips from the word of God which is then coupled with miracles and healing. The gifts (plural) of healing also bring restoration into the lives of believers as well as releasing healing miracles as signs of the kingdom. Helps and administrating (helmsmanship or governing) are necessary gifts to enable the camp to function efficiently. Various kinds of tongues is an interesting last one mentioned and maybe highlights the importance of heavenly language in our own prayer times and in releasing heavenly communication in our times together. This list is not exhaustive and other gifts may come into play at times.

**THE PRACTICES AND PRIORITIES**

The base camp must be a place of God's presence above all else, where the atmosphere of heaven is experienced. We build on the foundations and core values we outlined in chapter two.

Here are four main priority practices of the base camp:

1.  **Worship and prayer in the Spirit (Philippians 3:3; Ephesians 6:18; Jude v20; Romans 8:26).**

    Here we reform a house of prayer, clearing out what doesn't belong, lifting up childlike praise, and bringing healing to the blind and lame (see Matthew 21:12-16). In this worship, we are kindling a fresh fire of love and adoration of the Lord, and in praying with the Spirit we are calling in his kingdom on earth as it is in heaven. With this focus, the beauty of the

Lord feeds and fills our hearts, and the Spirit's revelation fuels and furthers our praying. In this atmosphere, prayer is a delight, not a duty, and is motivated by grace, not guilt. The Spirit's revelation enables our praying to be proactive and precise. This worship and prayer will help clear the way for and establish an open heaven where we can receive much more from the Spirit. It will also bring a disruption of the works of darkness in the area as Paul's ministry did in Ephesus. Like Elisha, we will receive revelation of the intentions of the enemy and be able to counter them effectively (see 2 Kings 6:8-12).

In our times of worship and intercessory prayer, we take time to behold the Lord in worship, listen and receive revelation from the Holy Spirit, and call forth on earth what is being revealed and released from heaven.

2. **Equipping all God's people for the work of the kingdom, that is to announce good news, heal the sick, drive out demons, and disciple others in the ways of Jesus.**

There is a teaching role in this but also the preparing of the heart. We bring the Lord's healing to the wounds of the soul and vexations of the heart. There will be restoring work bringing people back to their true calling. The purpose of this equipping ministry is to make God's people fit in every way to run with the mission and purposes of God. The word 'equip' was also used for the mending of nets, and the setting and re-aligning of broken bones, so we both restore any broken-down relationships and align people into partnerships for mission.

We will run various courses to equip, activate, and release people in their ministry. To this end, we recommend our book, *Equipped: Activated and Released*.

3. **Release a fresh wave of miracles, healings, signs, and wonders.**

There is a great need to re-emphasise what were a major aspect of Jesus' ministry and a key part in the expansion of the church in the book of Acts. There is also a great requirement to release these works out from the confines of the believing community and into the wider society. Like Stephen who was "full of grace and power, was doing great wonders and signs among the people" (Acts 6:8), we also need to let loose healing as a sign of the kingdom of God. Such signs bring great opening and opportunity (e.g., Acts 8:4-8) but also opposition. We have witnessed many such signs of the kingdom over the years where people have come out of wheelchairs, tumours have suddenly disappeared and been medically shown to have gone, and various other healing miracles. These have often shifted people from an unbelieving position to faith in Jesus. This is not reserved for a few 'special saints' but is for all of God's people who will take him at his word, believe, get equipped, and step out in faith and obedience.

4. **Send out workers into the Lord's harvest field, our mission arena.**

We don't want to keep people at the base camp longer than necessary, but we want to release them and send them out to share the good news, demonstrate the kingdom of God, disciple people, and form simple churches around those disciples. Others may continue with existing churches bringing a new vibrancy and the life of the Spirit into their situations. There can and should be a continuing relational connection with the base camp for mutual encouragement and any fresh equipping that is required later.

**SETTING UP AN APOSTOLIC BASE CAMP: WHAT IS NEEDED?**

**Base community:** A base camp needs a small base team that looks after supplies, deals with communications, and so forth. Likewise, our base camps require a small team or base community who will support the ministry in various ways – financially and organisationally and will gather regularly to worship, seek God's continued direction, pray, and encourage one another.

**Simple structure:** The structure must always serve the purpose and not become something in itself requiring maintenance. A structure that facilitates times for worship and prayer, equipping sessions, and times for personal development and restoration for individuals is what is required.

**Places to gather:** If available and suitable we might use a set place for a period of time, or equally we could use various locations. It is never about a building but ministry gifts operating. A place where we can worship with freedom, gather various sizes of groups, and minister privately to people is ideal.

**OPERATION OF MINISTRY GIFTS**

There will be some whose primary role is in the base camp and others who minister here and in other places. There will be some who come into the camp to bring an equipping contribution on specific occasions. And there will be small teams that go from the base camp to minister in other places and to form new base camps. These will resemble Paul's apostolic teams working together in harmony, valuing one another, complementing, and never competing, and giving credit and opportunity to the gifts of grace within each team player.

These Apostolic Base Camps can be set up all around the nations where they will raise the bar of expectation, raise the foundations, raise sons and daughters, and restore the apostolic mission. They will enable the breaking of new ground and the taking of territory from the domain of darkness. They will equip followers of Jesus to re-enter the mission arena with a new confidence in the Spirit's power, and so represent Jesus more fully and clearly.

# 6

# RE-ENGAGING THE MISSION ARENA

*The Great Commission is not an option to be considered; it is a command to be obeyed.*

Hudson Taylor

What if we could start again? We could ask this question in all sorts of areas of life – some might ask this concerning their marriage, their career path, or other roads that they have gone down. What if we could start the mission of Jesus Christ again in our land? What if we didn't have the baggage we created or church history has created? What might we do?

In Western Europe, we have had centuries of what can be called 'Christendom' where the influence of Christianity has permeated much of society and its values. This has dramatically decreased in recent decades. There has been the good, the bad, and the ugly in all this.

The good can be seen in the influence of moral values that helped the likes of the abolition of slavery. The bad is when it is assumed that someone born in a 'Christian' country is a Christian. The ugly is when a warped form of Christianity has been imposed on people, even on occasions with violence. So, there has been at times a wonderful impact and representation of Jesus and his ways. At other times, however, there has been a misrepresentation or even a distortion of Jesus, sometimes for political power, or financial gain. Often there has been over time a loss of the freshness of his river of life. We want to be captured afresh by the good news of Jesus and represent, that is re-present him more fully, clearly, and truly.


## HOW DO WE RE-ENTER THE MISSION ARENA?

First, in the Spirit of Christ, with his attitude and mind as outlined in Philippians 2:5-11, epitomised by humble obedience. Jesus did not come to dominate over nations but to spread the fragrance of his living presence in all grace and truth that would truly transform hearts. He did not seek to overthrow the Roman oppressors in Judea even though many hoped that would do just that. He came "not to be served but to serve, and to give his life as a ransom for many" (Mark 10:45). We must go in the same spirit.

Second, in the power of the Holy Spirit as that is what Jesus promised and proved so effective in Jesus' ministry and the mission of the early church. We need to throw off every hint of the wrong cessationist teaching that spiritual gifts of tongues, prophecy, and healing are not normative for today, and fully embrace the baptism and power of the Spirit for mission. This release of the power of the Spirit must be through the many not just a few where there is the danger they are seen as some sort of 'Christian celebrities.' This release of his power is never to justify or elevate us but to point to Jesus. That is why we must first cultivate his way of humility and trusting obedience.

Third, in developing a renewed mindset of being a missionary people at home rather than seeing ourselves primarily as a church people. How we see ourselves greatly affects our behaviour and manner of life. Now we are the church, but seeing ourselves as primarily a people who are based and settled in the forms of church life will not enhance our mission. However, seeing ourselves as the people of God on mission together will create a different pattern of thinking that will be more likely to launch us outward in a missional direction.

Fourth, by honestly questioning past methods and models. Are they fruitful, and even if they appear to produce fruit does it last? Are they founded in Scriptural truth and ways? We can appear effective using good selling methods or other less-than-honest ways, but we must follow Christ's ways and trust him for the lasting fruit that he promises of those who abide in him. We must be brave enough to reject some old unhelpful ways and wise enough to keep embracing some old but good ways. In truth, we need to get back to learning from the earliest ways.

Fifth, we need to re-enter this arena without presumption and assumption. We can no longer assume people have knowledge about God or the Christian faith. We cannot presume that people will have any sympathy with our faith but may even find great antagonism. We cannot presume people are looking to find God. However, we may discover that people are searching for spiritual truth, but they are not looking to the church for this. We will find that every person has a longing to be loved and to love and that the great themes of our faith like forgiveness, hope, peace, reconciliation, and justice are still most relevant but may need presented in fresh ways and not couched in 'evangelical jargon.'

Sixth, we re-enter as prepared and flexible people. We will travel some unfamiliar paths, and things are changing rapidly in our world. We need people who are prepared to walk continually listening to the leading of the Spirit, who are ready for whatever way the road may turn. In his book *Rising Tides*, Neil Cole says, "There are few leaders who can foresee the specifics of the future these days and prepare people to thrive in it. What we can do is prepare people for any future, rather than cast vision for our own idealised version of it."

Seventh, we prepare the ground in intercessory prayer. Out of the house of prayer established in the Apostolic Base Camp, we press into every area taking authority over the domain that darkness holds and bringing a release of the atmosphere of heaven. Out of heart expressions of worship, we wage war with heavenly weapons and gain godly wisdom to implement Christ's kingdom rule in the territory that we now occupy.

Finally, we re-enter with many questions on our lips as we continue to learn as we go:

How do we engage with people? How do we engage with the spiritual realm around us? How do we communicate and demonstrate the Good News here? How do we disciple these people? How do we form a meaningful church life? Who do we raise up as leaders and how do we train them? And lastly, how, and when do we multiply? We don't go thinking we know all the answers, but we go as continual learners.

We must re-enter the mission arena not because churches are closing, but because it is the command of Christ. While living a life that shows the distinction of one who belongs to the Lord, we must connect with those who don't yet believe. As we demonstrate the life of the kingdom, in love and service, in signs and wonders, we look for the opportunities to give an answer for the hope we have (1 Peter 3:15). We listen to the questions people might be asking rather than offering answers to the questions they are not asking.

There are many ways the Spirit of God can lead us to connect with people and communicate the good news of the kingdom to them. Here we will look at two passages that give us some principles and guidelines to apply in our situations.

**LUKE 10:1-9**

Jesus appoints and sends out 72 others (other than his twelve) while stating to them that the harvest is plentiful though there is a shortage in the workforce. He sends them and us:

1. In vulnerability – as lambs among wolves (v3) rather than where we feel strong or in control. Just as Jesus prepared for his mission by walking through the wilderness, we too will go through wilderness seasons where we are often stripped of any sense of self-sufficiency. We become aware of our weakness yet in this realise and release his true strength and sufficiency.

2. Without human provisions and resources (v4) – we don't actually need them, but we do need heavenly resources from the Holy Spirit. We are to travel light and not be sidetracked or distracted from our purpose.

3. To discover key connectors or 'people of peace' (v5-7) and enter their world. We carry the presence and

peace of Christ, and as we speak from his heart of peace we look for where this is welcomed and reciprocated. We will discover key individuals who have the manner and means of introducing us to whole circles of people.

4. Letting others do something for us (v7-8) which again can make us more vulnerable. In this, we show value for people, and they are often more open to listen to us. Jesus does this very thing with the Samaritan woman at the well where he first asks her for a drink (John 4:7). This then opens up a significant and life-changing conversation. Indeed, this woman is a person of peace who then introduces many others to Jesus.

5. Healing the sick and announcing the kingdom of God (v9). There is no shortage of illness and infirmity so plenty of opportunity. Three great areas of concern in many people's lives are relationships, health, and money. Jesus' ways of loving the Lord and loving your neighbour are the basis for healthy, life-giving relationships which have great bearing on our physical health. When we are truly present with people and interested in them, we can offer a simple blessing of healing into their souls and bodies.

Healing in Jesus' name flows well in the mission arena. We speak of the kingdom of God where Jesus addresses the great anxiety of many lives and offers the solution of seeking first the kingdom (see Matthew 6:25-33).

**ACTS 10:1-48**

This chapter of Acts describes a massive new departure and crossing over of cultural boundaries. Peter is called to go to a Gentile house and present Jesus to them which up to now the early church does not appear to have done.

What do we see in this monumental passage?

1.  The Holy Spirit is orchestrating the whole encounter along with angelic visitation (v1-7; 17-23). The Spirit is at work outside of us! We need to go and discover what he is already doing. There is more already happening than we may realise. We just need to look in the right place.

2.  Peter receives a revelation to break off his old mindset and break him into new territory and possibility (v9-16). We can be encumbered by ways of thinking and our internal bias which we may not even be aware that we have. We need to, like Peter, get out of the house of our familiarity and onto the

rooftop to pray, allowing the Spirit of God to break into our understanding. There are many places and people to go to that we may never have yet considered.

3. Peter then goes to Cornelius' world, into his home and sphere (v23-25). The angel could have explained the message to Cornelius or sent Cornelius to Peter, but God wanted to send Peter into the Gentile world. Rather than often pulling people away from 'their world' into our 'church world' we may need to form church around the new disciples helping them reach into the lives of those with whom they have been naturally connected.

When Peter enters Cornelius' home, we find some key principles unfold that we can learn much from:

1. Peter asks a question to gain understanding (v29). This is where we must not presume where people are at but start with questions. We need to develop the practice of asking good questions. These are often short and simple, yet have the ability to reach in deeply. Philip initiates conversation with the Ethiopian eunuch by asking him, "Do you understand what you are reading?" (Acts 8:30). We might ask,

for example, 'What is happening in your life just now?' or 'What is important to you at this time?'

2. Look for what God is already doing (v30-33). Peter listens as Cornelius recounts the angelic visitation. Several times we have talked with people who shared with us about dreams they have had that seem to have some meaning. This will often open up conversation around matters of the spiritual life and faith.

3. Once there is an opening then share the testimony of Jesus (v34-43). The opening here came through the angelic visitation, but it may also come through healings and other demonstrations of the kingdom of God. Be expectant, be observant, and be ready to make the most of every opportunity. As we partner with the Holy Spirit, we will not have to force things.

4. Make room for the Holy Spirit to work (v44-46). It is through the Spirit that people are born again and we must always let him supersede our efforts. In Acts 10, the Spirit interrupts Peter's preaching as he falls on the gathered group.

5. When people are clearly and demonstrably converted then baptise them into Christ and into the family of God (v47-48).

## A SPIRITUAL BATTLE

We recognise that there is a spiritual battle. The mission arena is under the influence of the domain of darkness and people's minds have been blinded by the god of this age (2 Corinthians 4:4). Paul speaks of our wrestling with spiritual forces of evil (Ephesians 6:12), and how he fought with 'wild beasts' at Ephesus (1 Corinthians 15:32), a clear reference to demonic powers. Yet he also states that 'a wide door for effective work' had opened in that city though there was much opposition (see 1 Corinthians 16:9-10). We engage as ambassadors and representatives of the kingdom of Jesus Christ expressing his authority in the following ways:

**Beholding and worshipping the King (Isaiah 33;17; Revelation 19:6):** We engage in warfare, but we do so in a God-centred and focused way. We war from a heart of worship. We refuse to be intimidated by the noise of the enemy but remain impressed by the greatness and majesty of the King of kings. We don't shout at the demons but raise a shout of praise to our God. We enter the fray of battle to the sound of songs of God's goodness, his steadfast love, and his faithfulness, even as Jehoshaphat's army did which led to a resounding victory as the Lord fought on their behalf (2 Chronicles 20).

**Seeking first the kingdom of God (Matthew 6:33):** Praying for the kingdom of God to come, that his life-giving reign will manifest on earth (Matthew 6:10). As Christ's kingdom advances the domain of darkness must retreat. Jesus didn't look for demons but his presence exposed them.

**Releasing the signs of the kingdom (Luke 10:9; 11:20):** Signs of the kingdom announce the arrival of the kingdom, and serve as an eviction notice to the powers of darkness in our land. Jesus said, "But if it is by the finger of God that I cast out demons, then the kingdom of God has come upon you" (Luke 11:20). This, he suggests, brings an overpowering of the strong man who is guarding his goods, and then those goods are plundered from him.

**Announcing the good news of the kingdom (Matthew 4:23; Acts 8:12):** We then make a confident announcement of the good news of the kingdom based on Christ's victory. The announcement of the good news will release the signs of the kingdom, and when the signs of the kingdom are displayed, they bring the declaration of the kingdom that has come and is coming.

**Inviting people to enter the kingdom (John 3:5):** Jesus issued the invitation to come. To come to him and find rest (Matthew 11:28), to come and see, that is discover who he is (John 1:39) and to come and follow him (Mark 1:17). Through Jesus we enter the kingdom realm of life and living. We invite people to change the way they think (repent), and how they see and define reality, and to come out of their wrong responses and past restrictions living under the curse, and come into the blessing and favour of God.

**Discipling them to live in the ways of the kingdom (Matthew 28:19-20):** Life in the kingdom of God is altogether different. We see differently having a whole new perspective. We need to learn to live in the ways of this kingdom, responding to the word and voice of God rather than reacting to people and the changing circumstances of our lives. We now live with an eternal perspective. This is the fullness of life that we are to disciple people into, where we live out of trust in the Lord, and therefore willingly and joyfully follow his commands.

Following the apostolic mission, partnering with the Holy Spirit and one another, we can learn to re-enter the mission arena beginning in our own town and sphere of influence, and then spreading ever wider in this unstoppable commission as we represent and re-present Jesus to everyone we can.

# 7

# REGENERATING SIMPLE CHURCH

*I believe in dreaming big and building small, one new
ekklesia of believers at a time. I believe the effectiveness of
any movement that makes lasting impact will be measured
by how effective it is in fostering a culture of discipleship
that thrusts its members out among the lost*
Floyd McClung

What on earth do we mean by 'church'? It has become a greatly overused and misunderstood term. We have many churches, many different names, many denominations of churches, and various styles of church. What does this term mean to most people in our nations? For many, it is a building, and usually an archaic one at that!

It is time to simplify and to re-form what has in some ways become formalised, stale, complicated, and burdensome. Life needs form, but when the form becomes more important than life something is very wrong, and soon the life will diminish and even die. Church needs some form but only what is necessary to enhance the life of God among us. Form itself is not wrong but when the structure becomes formalised it can crush life, restrict spontaneity, and dampen expression. To formalise is to give a definite structure to something, a structure that soon can become quite inflexible. We need to create simple church that has great flexibility.

There also needs to be a regeneration of existing churches where life may have been stifled and growth stunted. This may not be an easy task and can be met by resistance at times. Other times there is a willingness to change some things but maybe not for the fundamental shift that may be required. However, there is always hope for new life, a new vibrancy, and a fresh work of the Spirit.

For a great harvest though we will need many, many new churches to be birthed with the DNA of multiplication within them. Birthing a new church doesn't mean starting a church service somewhere. It is about finding and forming disciples who will be a worshipping family of faith on a road of mission together. For this to be fruitful we need to have the aims and focus of discipleship and reproducing ourselves at the heart of who and what we are.

It doesn't have to be hard toil. We don't necessarily need buildings or budgets or professional clergy. These may even hold us back. It needs to be lightweight. Mike Breen says of the New Testament churches, "The household churches were lightweight enough to be able to be planted in almost any context, and the power of their kingdom ministry led to a reputation for healing and deliverance." We need a format of life that is mission-effective.

The aim isn't to grow one large local church but to reproduce and multiply, so the emphasis is on minimising size and maximising discipling people. Whatever we do has to be reproducible by our people. We may need to reduce to reproduce.

No set model of church life must be adopted. There is freedom for different expressions, not because we have divided over some issue, but because we are looking to bring different groups and types of people into meaningfully following Jesus and reproducing themselves.

**KEYS OF SIMPLE CHURCH:**

**Life-giving:** Jesus gives us life in all its fullness so the corporate life of his family must always be life-giving in all it does. When church structures, forms, and programmes become too demanding it can feel like they are sucking the life out of us. Some people have disengaged from church for this very reason. The Spirit of Jesus is life-giving, and we need to be a people among whom that life can flow freely among us.

**Simple:** We have used this term a lot so far! No term is ideal but as we wrestle the word 'church' free from its unhelpful connotations we need to find some other language. The term 'simple' means to keep the form of church to as little as is meaningful and effective in our aim of making many disciples who live out the commands of Jesus. We must be deliberate about remaining simple as we have an inherent tendency to complicate things. Charles Kridiotis in his book *Simply Kingdom: Simple Church* says, "Simple church includes any group of disciples where Jesus is Lord and where his mission is central to their ethos."

**High on relationships:** If we are family then relationships are of the utmost importance. We need our form to enable the expression and development of our relationship with God and with each other. The New Testament presents many ways in which we can express loving relationships. Here's a list of twenty such exhortations:

1. "Love one another" (John 13:34)

2. "Be devoted to one another in brotherly love" (Romans 12:10)

3. "Honour one another above yourselves." (Romans 12:10)

4. "Live in harmony with one another" (Romans 12:16)

5. "Accept one another, then, just as Christ accepted you" (Romans 15:7)

6. "Instruct one another." (Romans 15:14)

7. "Serve one another in love." (Galatians 5:13)

8. "Carry each other's burdens" (Galatians 6:2)

9. "Be patient, bearing with one another in love." (Ephesians 4:2)

10. "Be kind and compassionate to one another" (Ephesians 4:32)

11. "Forgiving each other" (Ephesians 4:32)

12. "Speak to one another with psalms, hymns, and spiritual songs." (Ephesians 5:19)

13. "Submit to one another out of reverence for Christ." (Ephesians 5:21)

14. "In humility consider others better than yourselves." (Philippians 2:3)

15. "Encourage one another daily" Hebrews 3:13)

16. "Spur one another on toward love and good deeds." (Hebrews 10:24)

17. "Confess your sins to each other" (James 5:16)

18. "Pray for each other." (James 5:16)

19. "Offer hospitality to one another without grumbling." (I Peter 4:9)

20. "Build each other up" (I Thessalonians 5:11)

**Low on maintenance:** The burdens that can come with maintaining forms, buildings, and programmes need to be cast off! Keeping form simple will help with this, and allow more time and energy for relationships and mission. There is a pressure to keep certain things going that can weary people and take up much of our resources.

**Discovery and obedience-based discipleship:** We have at times majored in giving information when we need revelation, understanding, and means of expressing what we learn. People learn more and become more effective by discovering and doing. There is also little value in teaching people beyond their obedience. If people are not putting into practice what they already know of the ways of Christ, then they are not ready to receive more teaching in other areas.

**Flexible:** When form takes over, churches become set in their ways. Some ways are good and others are unhelpful. We need to be ready to go where the Spirit leads, to change direction at times, and to follow unfamiliar paths to the greatest fruit. Simpler and smaller expressions of church can be much more flexible.

**Easily reproducible:** What we do and how we meet must be easy to replicate so we multiply and fill the land. Whatever we do must be simple and clear enough that it can be reproduced by the people we train.

## WHAT COULD IT LOOK LIKE?

We want to meet regularly where we gather together to share our lives and our food, to worship the Lord, to hear and explore his Word, and to pray for one another and for God's kingdom to come on earth as in heaven. As we gather, we encourage, equip, and enable each other to spread the good news of Jesus more effectively. Neil Cole in his book *Church 3.0* says, "Instead of seeing church as something that serves its people, church becomes people who serve God, one another, and a hurting world." Church is not about putting on a service or providing a range of services to pander to a consumer mentality.

There needs to be a fundamental shift in the way we view what church is and in the way we see its purpose. The church is a fellowship of believers. The word *koinonia* which is translated as fellowship means to share in a common life and purpose. A simpler, smaller gathering enables this far more easily than a large event type of gathering. Though small in size the aim is to grow and multiply.

These simple churches are much more than 'house groups' which are often an optional extra in the life of a church. Even where there is a strong emphasis and attendance of house groups, they rarely have a vision for multiplying themselves. It is never only about having smaller forms of church that can be more relational and flexible, but always about being a people whom the Spirit of God can move among and through in the mission of Christ to see more and more people becoming disciples of Jesus.

**BIRTHING NEW CHURCHES**

Can we do this? Who can do this?

We are raising up sons and daughters who will become fathers and mothers. Fathers and mothers give birth! Creating a simple church like we have been describing does not necessarily require years of theological study or formal training. If we are to see a movement of God in our land, we may not have time for that. Out of the Apostolic Base Camp, hundreds and thousands of sons and daughters who are ready to become fathers and mothers will be launched. They are sent out by the Holy Spirit, abiding deeply in a living relationship with Christ, the word of God dwelling richly within them, worshipping together, praying, announcing good news, demonstrating the kingdom of God, discipling those they engage with, bringing them to faith, baptising them, and forming these simple churches that are always preparing for and looking to reproduce.

They are not cut loose but they are free to run. They will stay in relationship with the Apostolic Base Camp, returning when necessary for further equipping, and gathering on occasions with the larger group of believers for worship, inspirational preaching, and celebration. These larger gatherings are to serve the purpose and mission of the smaller, simple churches, not the other way around. As numbers grow, we must resist the temptation to return to larger gatherings being our primary concern.

## REPRODUCING OURSELVES: THE DYNAMIC OF MULTIPLICATION

Over time churches have experienced subtraction, division, addition, and on too few occasions multiplication. When I was first called to lead a church there was division! About one-third of the people left, and others soon followed. I felt like I had an unfortunate gift for shrinking the church! Thankfully, some addition followed, and over the years we have even seen some multiplication. Too many churches in Western nations in recent times have witnessed loss and even closure. In that scenario, we can understandably be all too delighted with some addition, no matter how small. But we are not blessed to be fruitful and have a bit of addition to us, but to be fruitful and multiply. Addition can seem easier and quicker. Multiplication can have a long runway before take-off. Yet it is only through multiplication that we will see the level of harvest that the Lord is opening up to us.

Maybe our biggest obstacle here is that most of us are unaccustomed to multiplication and therefore do not understand its spiritual dynamic. We might look at how little we have and how great the task is and feel overwhelmed or try to find a reasonable solution. We find this happening in the account of the feeding of the 5,000 (Luke 9:11-17). The disciples rightly recognise the need of this great crowd as we might recognise the spiritual need of our nations. They come up with a sensible idea to send the people off to find food and lodging. But Jesus sees something altogether different. He sees what is possible in a different realm. He invites and challenges his disciples to be involved in this with him, as he outrageously says to them to give the crowd something to eat.

We learn three keys from Jesus' approach to this situation:

1. He takes and uses what they have even though it is minuscule in the face of the need. We must not be put off by how little we may seem to have or how few people are with us.

2. Jesus tells the disciples to arrange the crowd into groups of around fifty. When we think about the harvest, we might long to reach 5,000 people but not know even how to begin. However, maybe we

could reach fifty or even five. When we think about birthing new simple churches, we need to think about a few that can multiply year by year. Once we start multiplying, the numbers start quite small but soon begin to grow exponentially.

3. He blesses and breaks up what they have, the loaves and fish. As Jesus blesses us, he also breaks us up out of our confines so we can spread and multiply.

**RELEASING A MOVEMENT**

What do you see? What do you want to see?

We want to see a movement of God across our lands, watering the dry places, spreading the fragrance of Jesus, and filling the earth with the Father's glory!

We are seeking to answer the question: What will it take?

It requires a risk – which is how John Wimber used to say that we spell faith! We live in an increasingly risk-adverse society but we must be a people willing to risk it all for the greater prize. To take a risk is not necessarily to be reckless but it does mean to step out in obedience to the voice of God. It requires that we have a heart for letting loose that releases and permits the people of God who have been equipped and activated to step into their calling. It means trusting them, but above all trusting the Lord of the harvest who said to ask him to thrust out workers into his harvest field. Those who are motivated by the love of Christ need to be mobilised to go and act without our direct supervision in every detail. Only then will we get a movement that will significantly affect and impact our nations.

In 2004 we birthed the first Healing Room in Scotland in response to a word from the Lord to release healing as a sign of his kingdom in our land. It was a simple concept. The vision was to make the healing, saving power of Jesus available and accessible to the people of our towns and cities. We would run a training course to equip believers to minister Christ's healing, then identify, spend time with, pray over, and appoint leaders for a local 'room' who would form a team of volunteers. We would find places to meet in, often being given the use of premises free of charge. A time would be set to open weekly to the public, and though responses varied across the country many people experienced healing in various ways, and significant numbers of people came to faith in Jesus Christ.

Our team members were being discipled all the time. They grew in their understanding as they put into practice what they were learning. They grew in maturity and wisdom through experience and obeying the commands of Jesus to heal the sick, cast out demons, and announce the good news of the kingdom of God. As they met, the team spent time worshipping the Lord together, they prayed together and for one another, and then ministered in partnership with the Holy Spirit to those who came to them. This was not a local church but had many of the features and functions of one.

The number of rooms soon multiplied throughout the nation. As we grew in numbers, we would gather volunteers from various rooms in an area to meet once a month to worship, tell testimonies, and receive further teaching, encouragement, and inspiration from God's Word. Twice a year we would gather all the local leaders for a similar purpose as the volunteer gatherings, and we would hold an annual conference for a greater level of input and energising in the Spirit. The ministry developed other avenues of expression as we ministered in prisons and psychic fares.

We believe many of the same principles and practices could now be applied to a movement of simple churches spreading throughout the nation. We would train up leaders releasing them to birth a simple church. Then gather the churches of any given area to meet every month or two in a larger setting. Here we bring input and encouragement to keep focussed on our mission of making disciples. We would keep investing in leaders and training new leaders to birth more simple churches. An annual gathering would be held to tell the stories of all that God is doing and to celebrate this together.

This does not require big budgets, full-time staff, or purchasing buildings. Organisation is kept to a minimal level to keep the ministry moving forward. We invest in people who we then release into the ripe fields to be fruitful and multiply.

# 8

# RECEIVING FRESH BREATH

*He (Jesus) breathed on them and said to them,*

*"Receive the Holy Spirit."*

John 20:22

We can set our sails but unless the wind blows, we won't move. On the other hand, if we don't set our sails and the wind does blow then we won't go anywhere either. So, we are setting the sails as we raise the bar of our expectation, as we raise up the foundations, raise and equip sons and daughters, restore the apostolic mission, recreate apostolic base camps, re-engage the mission arena, and regenerate a simpler and more reproducible church. Now we need the mighty rushing wind of God's Spirit to come. We are not asking God to come blow on 'our thing' but we are raising these sails in obedience to his word and what he is telling us, in full expectation of a fresh moving of the Spirit.

We can have great ideas and vision, and have everything in place, but without the Spirit, we are like the army in Ezekiel before the breath comes (see Ezekiel 37:1-10). Ezekiel prophesied as commanded by the Lord and the dry bones came together. Sinews and flesh came upon them and skin covered them, but most tellingly he states in verse 8, "But there was no breath in them." So, Ezekiel had to prophesy once more. He had prophesied correctly as the Lord had instructed him, but he had to press in and speak again, this time to the breath. The breath of the Spirit entered them and they lived and stood up, an exceedingly great army.

We can feel that we have followed the Lord's instruction but not seen the fulfilment of his promise. We can't afford to stop short, or sit down discouraged, or feel sorry for ourselves. We mustn't fall into complaining or grumbling. We must seek the Lord afresh, listen for his word to us, and go again. Prophesy again calling forth the wind of the Holy Spirit.

We both pray for this fresh outpouring and pray so that we will be ready for the outpouring so that we can flow with him as he comes. As we humbly seek the Lord and call on his name, so in these times our hearts are tenderised and prepared to receive and run with the answer to our prayer. Our hearts can become dulled or calloused through discouragement and disappointment, which can form unbelief in us. We keep our hearts tender towards the Lord by gazing upon his beauty. As we do this, we rejoice in him, pray continually, and give thanks in all circumstances (1 Thessalonians 5:16-18). Posturing our hearts in worship keeps us tender and sensitive to the Lord and his leading.

In a previous season, a group of us set ourselves to pray for an outpouring of the Holy Spirit upon us and to flow into our community. We met and prayed two evenings a week for four years with that one prayer on our lips. The Lord poured out his living waters graciously and generously resulting in some wonderful breakthroughs and changing the course of our lives and ministry. In these times of worship and prayer, the anointing of the Spirit would flow gloriously upon us, and two hours would go by as if it were just a few minutes.

Jesus said, "When the Holy Spirit has come," not if he might come. He described him as "the promise of my Father" and God fulfils his promises. So, we pray, 'Come, Holy Spirit, fall afresh on us, fill us, empower us, carry us in your river that brings life wherever it flows.' May the power of the Most High overshadow us bringing to birth fresh expressions of the life of Jesus, the Son of God (see Luke 1:35).

May we respond as Mary (Luke 1:34-56) that we might move from prophetic promise to fulfilment:

1. Mary seeks understanding (v34). May we be asking the best questions that help us gain an understanding of the clearer and fuller purposes of God.

2. Mary believes the word that was spoken to her even though it transcended human possibility (v38, 45). May we display a similarly outrageous faith.

3. She re-positions herself quickly (v39). Some may need to re-position themselves out of unbelieving circles to where they find faith, like-mindedness, and similar passion. We cannot afford to let the seed of faith be crushed or stolen, or the fire of the Lord be extinguished.

4. Mary links with one with a similar word (v36, 40, 56). We can feel alone and isolated, especially when we

are forerunning a fresh work of the Lord. There is great strength for us in finding and linking with others who are hearing something similar in the Spirit.

5. She receives confirmation of the word given to her (v41, 44), and the two women spark off each other in the Spirit. This is a wonderful picture of those carrying the prophetic seed of promise connecting to each other, recognising what each is carrying, and stirring and stoking the fire within one another.

6. Mary sings and creates a timeless song as the Spirit gives her language and expression of the revelation and understanding she has received (v46-55). Moves of God have always and will continue to produce new songs.

## AN OUTPOURING ON OUR NATIONS

The outpouring of the Spirit on the day of Pentecost continues to pour out. It is inexhaustible and unstoppable! This river of living water is always seeking lives that are ready to receive and run with it. The river finds hearts of humility that are set towards the Lord. The expressions of Acts 2:17-21 manifest in and through us as sons and daughters who prophesy, and who move in the signs and wonders of the kingdom of God. The final promise of those verses is 'that everyone who calls on the name of the Lord shall be saved.' This outpouring is going somewhere. It is flowing out to fulfil the heart of the Father to redeem, reconcile, save, and make new.

James 5:18 says of Elijah, "Then he prayed again, and heaven gave rain, and the earth bore its fruit." We need to pray again. As we may have witnessed God moving in power before, we still need to press in and pray again that the rains of his Spirit will water the land and bring forth the fruit of salvation. We need a second wind that will energise us afresh. Zechariah 10:1 calls us to, "Ask rain from the Lord in the season of the spring (latter) rain." The early autumn rains soften and prepare the ground for planting, and the spring rains, also known as the latter rains, swell the corn as it matures and is readied for reaping. Ask and it shall be given to you.

## WHAT'S NEXT?

We don't want to see a quick, flash in the pan, move of the Spirit. We want to see lasting fruit, a longevity that fulfils all that God desires for us.

Three things are necessary:

1. Steward the grace we have been given. Paul speaks of "the stewardship of God's grace that was given to me for you" (Ephesians 3:2). It is a gift of his grace, but as recipients of the gift we have the responsibility to take care of it, to put it to its correct use, and help bring about its fullest potential.

2. Sustain this move of God's Spirit by responding openly to him and giving him his place at all times. How easily a move can grind to a halt as people try to take control, and thereby quench the Spirit, or we reject part of what God is doing because it doesn't fit with our preconceived ideas or makes us uncomfortable. We must remain humble and obedient.

3. Increasing his deposit in us (Matthew 25:29). We don't sustain the moving of the Spirit to keep it at a level we like. His moving will always be increasing beyond us and we need to increase with him. Whether he gives us a small measure or a large one we must put it to use. As we use well what he entrusts to us we will be given more. He wills to give us an abundance.

As we are filled afresh, the Spirit in us will raise our expectations further. He will bring us into the greater fullness of Christ, raising us to stand to full height as sons and daughters of the king. He longs to and will lead us out to make Jesus known in works, wonders, and words. He will flow through us as we impart this gift of the Spirit to those who come to faith.

Let us raise the sails and may his mighty rushing wind blow!

*Lord Jesus, breathe afresh upon us. Fill us, empower us, and carry us on the wind of your Holy Spirit to be fruitful and to multiply, and fill our lands with the Father's glory!*

**Further reading and resources:**

The All Nations Storehouse has a large amount of video and written resources relating to discipleship, leading home churches, mission, healing, and much more.

www.anstorehouse.org


**Some books for further reading:**

Addison, Steve. *Acts and The Movement of God* and *Pioneering Movements*

Breen, Mike. *Building a Discipleship Culture* and *Leading Kingdom Movements*

Broweleit, Matt. *Out of the 4th Place*

Chan, Frances. *Letters to the Church*

Choudhrie, Victor. *Greet the Church in Your House*

Cole, Neil. *Church 3.0; Organic Church* and *Rising Tides*

Galanos, Chris. *From Megachurch to Multiplication*

Moran, Roy. *Hybrid Church* and *Spent Matches*

Neighbour, Ralph W. Jr. *Christ's Basic Bodies*

Sanders, Brain. *Microchurches*

Sawka, Ronald. *Apostolic Centres*

Trousdale, Jerry. *Kingdom Unleashed*

Uppal, Steve and Esther. *Revival ready*


**Books by Steven and Helen Anderson:**

The following are all available from www.amazon.co.uk
*Releasing Healing, The Day That Changed My Life, Life to the Full, Discovery Questions,* and *Equipped: Activated and Released.*


Steven and Helen Anderson have been involved in a variety of Christian leadership roles since 1987. Steven was a pastor in Glasgow from 1987 -1999, before he and Helen together formed Prayer for the City, a ministry seeking to bring united, envisioned, and sustained prayer for transformation. In 2004 they pioneered Healing Rooms in Scotland which they led as National Directors for 10 years, seeing 50 rooms open and operating across their nation. Steven and Helen have ministered in several nations through the work of Healing Rooms.

Steven and Helen's heart is to see people come into true freedom in Christ, be made whole through the Father's love, and equip them to live in the kingdom of God, activating their gifts and ministries in preparation for a fresh outpouring of God's Spirit.

Contact information: E-mail: stevenjohnanderson1@gmail.com

Facebook: https://www.facebook.com/breakthroughinthespirit

Printed in Great Britain
by Amazon